Edward William Brabrook

The Royal Society of Literature of the United Kingdom

A brief Account of its Origin and Progress

Edward William Brabrook

The Royal Society of Literature of the United Kingdom
A brief Account of its Origin and Progress

ISBN/EAN: 9783337071530

Printed in Europe, USA, Canada, Australia, Japan

Cover: Foto ©ninafisch / pixelio.de

More available books at **www.hansebooks.com**

The Royal Society of Literature of the United Kingdom.

A BRIEF ACCOUNT OF ITS ORIGIN AND PROGRESS.

Prepared, under the direction of the Council,

BY

EDWARD W. BRABROOK, C.B., F.S.A.

Vice-President and Treasurer R.S.L.; President of the Anthropological Institute; Chief Registrar of Friendly Societies.

SECOND EDITION.

LONDON:
ASHER AND CO., 13 BEDFORD STREET, W.C.

1897.

Royal Society of Literature.

A BRIEF ACCOUNT OF ITS ORIGIN AND PROGRESS

In October, 1820, in "accidental conversation," a "person" who can be identified as Thomas Burgess, then Bishop of St. David's, afterwards of Salisbury, suggested to another the advantages which might be expected from the institution of a Society of Literature, somewhat resembling the French Academy of Belles Lettres. The suggestion was communicated to Sir Benjamin Bloomfield, and by him to King George the Fourth, who had but recently ascended the throne.

On the 2nd November the Bishop received His Majesty's command to attend at Carlton House to discuss the matter, and was directed to draw up a plan in elaboration of a general outline which he had previously submitted. He also made a respectful communication on the matter to the Secretary of State for the Home Department.

His Majesty became the Patron of the proposed Society, and assigned out of his Privy Purse the annual sum of 1,100 guineas to be applied in pensions of 100 guineas each to ten Royal Associates, and (as at first proposed) in a premium of 100 guineas for a prize dissertation. Bishop Burgess's biographer (Harford, p. 344) says that the King told the Dean of Salisbury that this munificence on his part arose from a misconception of the Bishop's. The King had intended to give £1,000 down, and an annual subscription of £100 only; but the Bishop proclaimed so widely the King's munificent intention of giving 1,000 guineas a year, and it was commented on in the Press in terms so eulogistic, that he was obliged to acquiesce in it, and did so cheerfully.

By May, 1822, a sufficient number of subscribers had associated themselves with the proposed Society to enable a provisional Council to be formed under the presidency of the Bishop, who met the obstacles opposed to the formation of the Society with his characteristic perseverance.

One plausible objection raised was, that under cover of literary discussion, incessant controversies on political and religious topics might be raised, and the Society, under its Royal patronage, made an instrument of attack or defence of particular sects or parties according to the passions or interests of individual members.

It was not till the 2nd June, 1823, that a Constitution and Regulations were ready to be submitted by the Bishop to the King, and received his Majesty's approval under his sign manual, communicated to his Lordship by Sir William Knighton.

On the 17th June the first meeting of the Society, convened by public advertisement and by circular, was held at the house of the Literary Fund in Lincoln's Inn Fields. At this meeting the Officers and Council of the Society were elected as follows:

President: The Bishop of St. David's (afterwards of Salisbury).

Vice-Presidents: The Bishop (C. J. Blomfield) of Chester (afterwards of London); the Lord Chief Justice (Abbott; afterwards Baron Tenterden); the Right Hon. J. C. Villiers; the Right Hon. Sir Gore Ouseley; the Hon. G. Agar Ellis; Sir James Mackintosh; the Ven. Archdeacon Nares; Colonel William Martin Leake.

Treasurer: Archibald E. Impey.

Librarian: The Rev. H. H. Baber.

Secretary: The Rev. R. Cattermole.

Council: The Marquis of Lansdowne, Lord Grenville, Lord Morpeth, Sir Thomas Acland, Bart., Sir Alexander Johnstone, Francis Chantrey, Taylor Combe, the Rev. G. Croly, James Cumming, William Empson, the Rev.

Dr. Gray, Prince Hoare, William Jerdan, the Ven. Archdeacon Prosser, the Rev. Dr. Richards, the Rev. Charles Sumner.

At this time the Society appears to have consisted of about 120 Members, the three Royal Dukes, of York, Clarence, and Cambridge, having been the first Fellows enrolled after the King, and each having contributed a composition of 100 guineas. Lord Bexley, the venerable Bishop of Durham (Shute Barrington), and the Rev. Lewis Way made similar liberal donations to the funds of the Society.

Two guineas was fixed by the regulations as the minimum annual subscription, but a great number of the Fellows subscribed five and ten guineas each. Among these were the Dukes of Newcastle and Rutland, and several Bishops and Peers.

The first Council Meeting was held on Saturday, 21st June, 1823, at the apartments of the Rev. H. H. Baber in the British Museum; and the first Ordinary Meeting on 5th November, when Granville Penn, Fellow of the Society, read an account of an unknown manuscript of 1422, illustrating the last declaration of Henry the Fifth. The reading of the paper was not completed until the meeting of 19th November.

The Council proceeded, among its first duties, to the election of the ten Royal Associates, who were to be persons of distinguished learning, authors of some creditable work of literature, and men of good moral character. Those selected were—

Samuel Taylor Coleridge.

Rev. Edward Davies, Author of Celtic Researches.

Rev. John Jamieson, D.D., F.R.S.E.

Rev. T. R. Malthus, F.R.S.

T. J. Mathias, F.R.S., F.S.A., Author of Runic Odes.

J. Millingen, F.S.A., Author of Peintures Antiques.

Sir Wm. Ouseley, LL.D., Author of Persian Miscellanies.

Wm. Roscoe, Author of Life of Lorenzo de' Medici.

Rev. H. J. Todd, F.S.A.

Sharon Turner, F.S.A.

The 100 guineas, intended to have been given as a prize for a dissertation on Homer, not having brought forth any essay worthy to receive it, had been converted into two medals worth 50 guineas each, which were awarded to Wm. Mitford—" having completed a History of Greece from the earliest ages to the death of Alexander the Great, in which he has evinced great industry and learning, clear and acute reasoning, and an intimate knowledge of the practical operation of the various institutions, that form the component parts of free government, on the happiness and improvement of mankind, and having thereby largely contributed to raise the literary character of this kingdom"—and Angelo Maï, "late Librarian at Milan, and at present Librarian to the Vatican, having performed most important services to

Literature by the discovery and publication of many unpublished works of some of the greatest writers of antiquity."

By the regulations it was provided that every Royal Associate should, on his admission, choose some branch of literature, and that it should be his duty to communicate to the Council, once a year at least, a disquisition or essay on some point relative to that branch of literature so chosen by him. Sharon Turner chose "Philology and History," and contributed papers which were read on 3rd and 17th December, 1823, and 7th January and 21st April, 1824, on the mutual resemblances discoverable in the languages of nations not related to each other by known origin or by any geographical antiquity; illustrated by a comparison and classification of the terms, both simple and compound, used by various ancient and modern nations to express the numerals 1 and 2, and the relation of "mother."

At the next meeting, on 21st January, 1824,

a paper was read on the counterfeit madness of Hamlet, and the motive which induced him to assume the appearance of distraction, by Thomas Bowdler, not a Fellow of the Society, but a person who has acquired a certain amount of unenviable literary fame as the castrator of Shakespeare's Plays.

Sir William Ouseley, Royal Associate, chose as his branch of literature, " Oriental history, geography, and antiquities," and fulfilled his obligation by reading on the 4th February a paper on the River Euphrates.

On 3rd and 17th March, Archdeacon Nares, V.P., read an historical account of the discoveries that have been made in palimpsest manuscripts, with especial reference to Maï's researches; and on 7th April, Mr. W. R. Hamilton, Fellow of the Society, and Envoy at the Court of Naples, communicated an account by Mr. Angell, architect, of the discovery of some Greek sculptures in the ruins of the temple at Selinus.

This was the Society's first year's work. It will not be necessary to record the work of subsequent years in the same detail.

At the Anniversary Meeting on 6th May, five of the Royal Associates were present and subscribed their obligations. Besides those already mentioned, the following subjects were selected :

S. T. Coleridge.—The relations of opposition and conjunction, in which the poetry (the Homeric and Tragic), the religion, and the mysteries of ancient Greece stood each to the other; with the differences between the sacerdotal and popular religion; and the influences of theology and scholastic logic on the language and literature of Christendom from the 11th century.

T. R. Malthus.—Political economy and statistics.

H. J. Todd.—Manuscripts, and especially those which relate to the literary history of this country.

Mr. Todd fulfilled his obligation on 19th January, 1825, by communicating a collection of passages of state under Queen Elizabeth and King James, written by Sir John Harrington; and on 16th March an account of a codex containing several Greek manuscripts belonging to the Patriarch of Jerusalem.

The other five Royal Associates afterwards selected the following subjects:

Mr. Roscoe, Literary history.

Mr. Davies, Celtic antiquities.

Dr. Jamieson, Ancient historical facts, rites, customs and languages.

Mr. Mathias, Italian literature.

Mr. Millingen, Archæology.

Mr. Millingen, in fulfilment of his undertaking, contributed on 16th February, 1825, an account of a coin of Metapontum. The Bishop remarked in his annual address for 1825, that the Royal Associates were, in effect, professors of those branches of literature which they adopted.

The Medals for 1825 were adjudged to James Rennell, F.R.S., "one of the first geographers of this or any other age or country, for his various and valuable illustrations and improvements of ancient and modern geography (particularly by his maps and memoir of Hindostan and the neighbouring countries, by his memoir of the geography of the peninsula of Hindostan, by his memoir of the geography of Africa, and by his geographical system of Herodotus)," and to Charles Wilkins, LL.D., for his researches in Sanscrit, and publication of the Bhagvat Geeta, Hitopadesa, and Sanscrit grammar.

Upon the 15th September, 1825, the Society received its Charter of Incorporation by the name of the Royal Society of Literature of the United Kingdom, in which its object is defined to be "the advancement of literature by the publication of inedited remains of ancient literature, and of such works as may be of great intrinsic value, but not of that popular character which usually claims the attention of publishers; by the promotion of discoveries in literature; by endeavouring to fix the standard as far as is practicable, and to preserve the purity of the English language; by the critical improvement of English lexicography; by the reading at public meetings of interesting papers on history, philosophy, poetry, philology, and the arts, and the publication of such of those papers as shall be approved of; by the assigning of honorary rewards to works of great literary merit, and to important discoveries in literature; and by establishing a correspondence with learned men in foreign countries for the purpose of literary inquiry and information."

During the Session 1825—26, Malthus, Coleridge, Sir Wm. Ouseley, Jamieson, Turner, Millingen, and Todd—seven out of the ten Royal Associates—fulfilled their obligation of reading papers; and at the anniversary of 1826 the Medals were awarded to John

Schweighäuser of Strasburg, and to Dugald Stewart, the moral philosopher.

About this time, though the Society had become a Chartered Society, it dropped the use of the term Fellow and the initials F.R.S.L., and adopted Member and M.R.S.L. instead.

In 1827 appeared the first portion of its Transactions, and also a fasciculus of hieroglyphics edited by Dr. Thomas Young. The Gold Medals were awarded to Walter Scott and Robert Southey; and those of 1828 to George Crabbe and Archdeacon William Coxe. In that year a second fasciculus of hieroglyphics appeared.

The Medals for 1829 were adjudged to William Roscoe, one of the Royal Associates, and to the Baron Antoine Isaac Silvestre de Sacy. In that year Vol. I. of the Society's Transactions was completed by the issue of Part 2. A paper was read before the Society which was noteworthy as having occupied five meetings—18th February, 4th and 18th March, and 1st and 15th April, 1829. It was by the Rev. F. Nolan, LL.D., Member of the Society, and was "On the antiquity and connection of the early cycles and their utility in settling the differences of chronologists."

The medals for 1830 were adjudged to Washington Irving and Henry Hallam. A final fasciculus of hieroglyphics was published in that year from the papers of Dr. Thomas Young, then deceased.

The following year was marked in the history of the Society by the loss of its munificent founder and patron, King George the Fourth, and the consequent discontinuance of the pensions to Royal Associates and of the Royal Medals. The roll of Royal Associates was also, for the first time, broken in upon by the death of the Rev. E. Davies. The year 1831 was also notable for the Society's entering into possession of its house or "college" in St. Martin's Place. It may be worth while at this point to state the position which the Society had acquired.

The Ordinary Members had increased to 244. In addition to the 9 remaining Royal Associates, there were 16 Honorary Associates. There were also 19 Honorary Members, of whom 8 were Englishmen and 11 Foreigners, making a total of 288. All these lists included many persons of distinction.

Among the Ordinary Members were included, besides the Royal Dukes, Manners-Sutton and Howley, Archbishops of Canterbury, and Vernon, afterwards Harcourt, Archbishop of York; the Dukes of Newcastle and Rutland; the Marquis of Lansdowne; the Earls of Belmore, Carlisle, Clare, Clarendon, Mountmorres, Munster, and Shrewsbury; the Viscount Goderich (afterwards Earl of Ripon, and President of the Society); the Bishops of Bath, Bristol, Carlisle, Chichester, Ely, Salisbury, Winchester, and Limerick; and the Lords Bexley, Carrington, Grenville, Kenyon,

Prudhoe (afterwards Duke of Northumberland), Tenterden, and John Townshend, besides several members of the House of Commons. Eminently aristocratic as the list of Fellows was, it was not exclusively so, for it included about 30 Fellows of the Royal Society, and about 40 of the Society of Antiquaries; while literature itself contributed to the list names such as those of Brayley and Britton, Crabbe and Croly, Hallam and Hartwell Horne, James and Jerdan, Nares and Nichols. I may be pardoned for mentioning one more name in this connection, that of Mr. Pratt, the first Registrar of Friendly Societies.

The list of Royal Associates has already been given, and it must be admitted that the Council made upon the whole an admirable selection of recipients of the Royal Bounty. Their task was a difficult one. As one of the Royal Associates had himself remarked (Mathias, "Pursuits of Literature," 16th edition, p. 140n), "Unless the province of encouraging letters, which should belong to the great, is administered with wisdom and discretion, it is more desirable that there were no encouragement at all." We may take the same writer's testimony as to the merits of some of those who afterwards became his colleagues. Of Sir Wm. Ouseley's "Persian Miscellanies" he says, "they abound with learned, pleasing, and curious information" (id., p. 202n). Roscoe's "Life of Lorenzo de' Medici" he describes as a phenomenon in literature, and says that it adds his name to the first rank of English classical historians. But, indeed, no testimony is necessary, for all the ten have written their names in enduring characters on the literature of their age. At the same time the well-meant endeavour to make them earn their pensions by an annual lecture on a defined subject was a comparative failure. The selection by the Associates of their "branches of literature" was in some cases eccentric. Take that of Malthus — "Political Economy and

Statistics." It produced papers of value, but certainly not of literary value. Bonar truly says ("Malthus and his Work," 1885, p. 263) that "he does little credit in them to his literary faculty; their composition is laboured and devoid of ornament." The ten Associates never all of them attempted to comply with the conditions of an annual paper, and had they done so the result would only have been to exclude from the consideration of the Society all papers by other Fellows, all fresh and original communications, in favour of a series of perfunctory because enforced treatises. The literary work which a man does because he is compelled to do it is not likely to be his best. As Coleridge, the most renowned and truly literary of the whole of them, says finely— ("Biog. Lit.," i., 238)—" Be not merely a man of letters. Let literature be an honourable augmentation to your arms; but not constitute the coat or fill the escutcheon." Upon the whole, therefore, we are inclined to think that, while the pensions to the Royal Associates were certainly well bestowed, and must have been beneficial indeed to some of the recipients, the Society itself was rather the gainer than the loser in its best interests by their discontinuance. It possibly lost some prestige by ceasing to be the almoner of Royal bounty, but it acquired more self-reliance, and its members were urged to greater efforts to establish and maintain its reputation.

It had been originally contemplated that, besides the ten pensions granted by the Crown, the Society should provide out of its own funds an equal number for ten other Associates; but its funds were never sufficient to enable it to make even a commencement of such a list, and we cannot bring ourselves to regret that the attempt was never made.

A list of Honorary Associates was, however, formed, including Bernard Barton (the Quaker poet), the Rev. H. Cary (the translator of Dante), George Crabb, George Croly, Dr.

Nathan Drake, Richard Duppa, the Rev. T. D. Fosbroke, William Jacob, F.R.S., the Rev. Samuel Lee (Professor of Hebrew at Cambridge), Dr. John Lingard (the historian), Dr. George Miller, Thomas Mitchell, James Montgomery (the poet), the Revs. James Parsons, Richard Polwhele, and Abraham Rees, D.D., F.R.S., Robert Southey (Poet Laureate), and Patrick Fraser Tytler. The qualification for an Honorary Associate, as prescribed by the by-laws, is the recommendation by three Members of the Council of the person proposed as one eminent for the pursuit of Literature.

The Society had also power by its by-laws to elect not more than 12 British subjects and an unlimited number of Foreigners as Honorary Members. It had elected the following 12 British subjects:

The Rev. Archibald Alison.
The Right Rev. Bishop Gleig.
William Magee, Archbishop of Dublin.
General Sir John Malcolm.

William Mitford (deceased).
James Rennell (deceased).
Henry Salt, F.R.S. (deceased).
Sir G. T. Staunton, Bart., F.R.S.
Dr. Charles Wilkins, F.R.S.
J. G. Wilkinson.
The Rev. Nicholas Wiseman (afterwards Cardinal).
Dr. Thomas Young (deceased).
And the following 11 Foreigners :
Bilderdijk, of Haarlem.
Champollion (le jeune), Paris.
Von Hammer, Austria.
Humbert, Geneva.
Alexander de Humboldt, Paris.
Letronne, Paris.
Maï, the Vatican.
Meyer, Brussels.
Rask, Copenhagen.
Raynouard, Paris.
Von Schlegel, Bonn.
The medallists have been already mentioned;

and, upon the whole, it may be asserted without fear of contradiction that the Society had, in this its first stage of existence during the lifetime of its Royal Founder, gathered into its ranks in one relation or another a large number of the most distinguished names that adorned the literature of that period. It had not been very active in publications; a single volume of Transactions and three fasciculi of Hieroglyphics having been all that it had produced. On the other hand, it had accumulated a considerable Building Fund (nearly £2,500), and had obtained an eligible site for its house, the entering into occupation of which may be taken as marking the commencement of the second period of its existence.

The first anniversary meeting of the Society in its own house, 4, St. Martin's Place (which was its home for 50 years), held on 4th May, 1832, took place in some circumstances of discouragement. On the previous 7th of December the Bishop of Salisbury had resigned the presidency, on the ground of advanced age and distance from London. After some not very strenuous deprecation, the Council accepted the resignation, nominating the Bishop Vice-President, and pursuant to the by-laws the interim presidency until the anniversary devolved upon the Duke of Rutland, as senior Vice-President. Lord Dover, however, consented to be President, and delivered an address in which, following a custom which Bishop Burgess, in the heat of controversy and in his anxiety to disprove Milton's authorship of the treatise " De Doctrinâ Christianâ," had adopted in the later years of his presidency, instead of commenting on the affairs of the Society, he discoursed on an interesting historical problem, that of the manner and period of the death of Richard the Second, King of England. He supported the view of Mr. Amyot, that Richard starved himself to death in Pomfret Castle. Another discouraging circumstance was, that no intimation had been received from the King of his intention to continue his brother's grants to the Royal Associates, and that therefore no payment could be made to them. The meeting, however, resolved to admit them to all the privileges of members without payment. A third, was in the fact that the building, as usual in such cases, had cost more than was expected, and that although Decimus Burton, the architect, had kindly foregone his commission, the Society had had to borrow £900 and owed £220 more. A fourth was the loss of many eminent members by death, exceeding the number of new members elected to fill their places. Among the deaths were Roscoe and Crabbe, Royal Medallists; the Archbishop (Magee) of Dublin; Bilderdijk and Champollion, Foreign Honorary Members; and the Society's Treasurer (Impey), and Foreign Secretary (De la Fite). The Council were able to announce, however, the issue of the first part of Volume II. of the Transactions; and by the 5th of June they received an intimation that the King would become an annual donor of £100 to the general fund of the Society.

At the next anniversary, in 1833, Lord Dover was unable through ill health to be present, but he sent for reading a " Dissertation on the Gowrie Conspiracy." The losses by death included Lord Tenterden and Sir James Mackintosh. Some valuable gifts to the Library were announced, including 116 volumes by Mr. L. H. Petit. The deposit with the Society of 700 volumes by Sir W. Ouseley, for reference by the members during his absence from England, was also acknowledged.

Shortly afterwards the Society had the misfortune to lose its second President, Lord Dover, by death, and the Bishop of Salisbury, who ranked as first Vice-President, again became President by virtue of the by-laws, *ad interim*, until the anniversary of 1834, when the Earl of Ripon was elected. No presidential address was then delivered, but in 1835 Lord Ripon referred to his predecessor in the following graceful terms :—" Your second President, Lord Dover, was snatched from his friends and from the activity of public life by an early death ; but not before he had given to the world more than one proof of his ardent love for literature, and had shown by his example that literary and historical pursuits are not incompatible with the more exciting engagements of political life. Lord Dover, in his addresses to you from this chair, gave an earnest of the interest he took in the welfare of this Society, and of his talents, had he been longer spared to us, for throwing light on the more obscure and difficult events of our early history. In paying this passing tribute to the memory of Lord Dover, I rejoice in doing justice to one with whose personal friendship I was honoured, whose talents I admired, and whose character I knew too well by experience not to respect and love." Other losses by death announced at the 1834 anniversary included Earl Granville, the Right Hon. C. P. Yorke, Jebb, Bishop of Limerick, and Sir John Malcolm. On the other hand, the Report of the Council contained one indication that the withdrawal of King George the Fourth's bounty was really a blessing in disguise, for it recorded that as many as 26 papers had been read before the Society during the Session—not one of them by a Royal Associate,—and thus gave evidence of a literary activity on the part of the Fellows of which there had been no signs in the Society's first period. At this time was commenced the excellent plan of issuing a short printed sheet of proceedings from time to time during the Session.

The obituary of 1835 included two Royal Associates — Coleridge and Malthus. Lord Ripon's eloquent obituary notice of the former may rightly be reproduced here.

A name to which our peculiar expressions of regret are due is that of Coleridge. When the Society was commissioned to elect ten eminent literary characters not in affluent circumstances as Royal Associates, Mr. Coleridge's circumstances and extraordinary merits combined to point him out to the Council as peculiarly worthy to be chosen of the number. He gratefully received, during seven years, this mark of His Majesty's regard for literary distinction; and it is to be lamented that, when that grant ceased, his bodily infirmities had rendered him incapable of practical exertion. Samuel Taylor Coleridge was the son of a clergyman in Devonshire. His father dying in his infancy, he was placed in Christ's Hospital, in London. Here the singular habits of the learned and meditative boy, for such he was, attracted the notice of Middleton, afterwards Bishop of Calcutta, at that time a Grecian in the school, who was the first to make Mr. Bowyer, then Head Master, acquainted with his remarkable abilities and acquirements. Coleridge immediately emerged from the obscurity of the lower forms, and in due time was transferred, with a high reputation, to Jesus College, Cambridge. He was one of Sir William Browne's medallists, and in other respects distinguished himself at the University, but quitted it without having graduated; and for some years afterwards, though possessed of faculties of the highest order, and an erudition almost universal, he exhibited that want of a fixed purpose and determinate will which commonly characterizes the youth of men of genius. Towards the close of the century Mr. Coleridge visited Germany, and resided for some time at Göttingen. Of this portion of his life some very agreeable memorials exist in the " Biographia Literaria; " and among its results, besides the Teutonic cast which it impressed upon much of his subsequent thoughts and language, we may consider the masterly version of Wallenstein, our first and best translation from the literature of modern Germany.

Mr. Coleridge afterwards went out to Malta in the capacity of Secretary to Sir Alexander Ball, Governor of that island. He returned home through Italy, and on his arrival in England resumed those local and friendly connections with Wordsworth and Southey, which occasioned these distinguished individuals to be commonly associated together in the literary history of our times by the name of the

"Lake Poets." Though by no means the fittest of the three—if any one of this gifted triumvirate could be pronounced fit—to fill a part in the busy world, Coleridge was the first to revisit the Metropolis. His powerful talents were now obscurely employed on the anonymous columns of the daily journals; and his glowing imagination, and the intricacies of his metaphysics, by turns electrified and lulled asleep the audiences of our literary and scientific lecture rooms. The inconveniences of such a mode of life, however, to a mind of his exquisite sensibility and peculiar habits, and in connection with bodily suffering, induced him to avail himself of an opportunity of escape, that promised retirement without total seclusion, and freedom to follow the master tendencies of his disposition, with the hope of employing his powers for the benefit of mankind. He accepted the offer of a generous friend to become an inmate in his house at Highgate; and from this time, till his lamented death, a secluded apartment, at once his study and his bedroom—commanding one of the most beautiful woodland prospects in the vicinity of London—became the scene of daily discourse, in which it is not too much to assert, that the most elevated and most splendidly endowed characters of ancient or modern times might have gladly borne an equal part.

To the question so often and triumphantly put to his admirers—" What has Coleridge done "?—time does not permit a full answer here. The very question, however, implies an admission of great acknowledged powers. It is true, that the number of his published works is soon summed up; but writings, embodying the profoundest elements of thought, are not fairly estimated by the number or bulk of the volumes they comprise; and if ever there was a writer whose sentences teemed with the combined wealth of the creative and meditative faculties—such a writer was Coleridge. But the best answer to that question will, it is hoped, be shortly given in the publication of some, at least, of the numerous manuscripts which he has left behind, especially of his long-promised volumes containing the entire system of his philosophy. In the meantime, passing over his more popular merits as a poet—in which character, however, he is second to no name among his contemporaries, not even to Wordsworth, who, " in his golden urn drew light " from Coleridge's thoughts, as from a perpetual fountain—we name his best known work, "The Friend," the noblest exposition of moral, political, and ideal philosophy which has appeared within a century and a half; and profoundly wise and eloquent "Lay Sermons;" the "Aids to Reflection," itself a school of discipline for all who would learn to think, and which, almost unread at home, is largely circulated and studied even in utilitarian America; the learned and beautiful Essay on the "Idea of the Church and State;" and, lastly, among those of his writings which he was himself in the habit of referring to with the most satisfaction, his Letters and Papers published in the "Morning Post and Courier" at the conclusion of the late war. In these latter productions (the collection and republication of which would be an important service to society) he emphatically foretold, as he also did often in conversation, the consequences of the undue growth of democratic influence, allied with the knowledge which includes power without any directing principle, and while he traced its causes to their remotest origin, he described the only effectual remedy for the evil, in the moral and intellectual improvement of all classes, by imparting a philosophical and biblical education to the higher orders, a religious one to those beneath. But, if we could fairly estimate "what Coleridge has done," we must take into account, and by no means as least in importance, the probable effects of his daily discourses with his friends. Time alone can enable the public to do justice to his writings : to do justice to his conversation it never will be able. It was not alone his "glistening eye," and animated features—radiant as they were with the glow of poetic inspiration; nor was it his silver tones, or his varied and expressive elocution, in which the enchantment of his discourse consisted. Equally severe in logical sequence, and as bright with the changing hues of poetry, but in form less widely discursive, and in style more expressive and simple, his best conversational Essays were perhaps in every respect superior to his written works; often has it occurred to the favoured hearer to sigh involuntarily at the close of his flowing periods, for some spell that could impart permanency to the words he had been listening to, in the full faith that a book would have been the result, to which no rival in wisdom and eloquence united exists among the rich products of genius!

And the hearers of Coleridge were many—not at once, but many in succession; it was rare if a visitor came and found Memnon silent: there was no need to wait for the rising of the sun; for the rays which woke that tuneful tongue arose from within, and were at all times obedient to the call of friendship, or the enquiry of the lover of truth. Hence, few persons of literary habits and taste, resident in London, or visitors, were wholly strangers to Coleridge's wonderful powers of discourse. The young and ingenuous were always greeted with a peculiar welcome. Not a few of these—the best and purest of the rising intellects of the age—were his affectionate pupils; their minds remain indelibly impressed and moulded by him, and thus "the bread," which from day to day he "cast upon the waters, will be found after many days," transferred by them into the living world of thought and literature, the seed of his wisdom is already scattered abroad, and will yet bear fruit in the busy scenes of social and active life.

It remains but to add a word in regard to that philosophical system, which was the subject of the meditations, the writings, and discourses of our venerable friend and fellow member, during the latter and better portion of his life.

His design was to establish a vital philosophy, with revelation for its basis, in the room of the mechanical, introduced among us at the Revolution, which he ever regarded, and emphatically described as the philosophy of death. His is the ideal philosophy, spiritualised and exalted by true religion; as we may suppose Plato would have taught it had Plato been a Christian, and lived in our times. Its grand principle is, that in the reality of the divine idea alone, as including the three self-subsistences of the Godhead, can we discover the ground of universal existence; and from this primal truth he evolves the unity of all real knowledge. The principle of this philosophy he has himself described as, "the referring of the mind to its own consciousness for truths indispensable to its own happiness;" while in the same place he explains its practical purposes to be, "to support all old and venerable truths, and by them to support, to kindle, to project the spirit; to make the reason spread light over our feelings, and to make the feelings, with their vital warmth, actualise our reason." It is a philosophy which recommends itself to all good and well-judging people, to the religious, by the light it reflects upon the truths of revelation, and by the depth, earnestness, and practical quality of the faith it encourages; to the philosophic mind, by its profundity, its justness, and the logical validity of its grounds; to the gentle and amiable, by the exceeding humanity and charity of its results; to the critical student, by its order and beauty; and to every man, as man, by the dignity it secures to his humanity, and the elevation it imparts to his hopes.

Malthus owed his reputation mainly to his remarkable work on the "Principles of Population," first published anonymously in 1797 and afterwards frequently reprinted and widely read. It may be said to have completely altered the public views with respect to the matters of which it treated; and it bore fruit with wonderful rapidity in the passing, without serious opposition, of a Bill for taking a Census, which had been denounced as impious 50 years before.

Other deaths in the same year were those of

Gray, Bishop of Bristol, and Prince Hoare, Foreign Secretary of the Royal Academy, who bequeathed to the Society the greater part of his library, and thus more than trebled the number of volumes in its possession. The activity of the Fellows was still well maintained, as many as 20 papers having been read at the meetings during the session.

Another Royal Associate, Mr. Mathias, died in 1835–36. He was a Fellow of the Royal Society and of the Society of Antiquaries, author of some critical works, and of a poem of a somewhat satirical cast upon the "Pursuits of Literature," very learnedly illustrated with notes; of a work on Runic Odes, and other publications. Ill-health and distance prevented him from selecting his special topic when the other Associates fixed upon theirs, but he finally notified that he would deal with Italian literature. The obituary of the same year comprised also Sparke, Bishop of Ely; Robert Lemon, deputy-keeper of the State Papers; and Dr.

Richard Valpy. The list of honorary members was increased by the names of van Westreenen van Tiellandt, of Holland, and d'Olénine, of Russia. The number of papers read in the year was 18.

The losses by death in the year 1836-37 were also heavy. They consisted of Bishop Burgess, the Society's founder and first President; Dr. George Richards, to whom the Society owes its Richards' fund, to be hereafter referred to; Sir Francis Freeling, Bart., and Sir John Byerley. These losses were referred to by Lord Ripon in the following terms :—

The Bishop of Salisbury was the author of many works of no ordinary merit, connected with the sacred profession to which he belonged; and he was remarkable for the zeal which he displayed for the advancement of Hebrew literature; the study of which, although not required as a test of fitness for the discharge of clerical duties, is of deep interest to a Christian community. Perhaps, however, there was no act in the Bishop's life which more claims our respectful notice than the zeal and liberality with which he commenced, continued, and completed the establishment, in the diocese of St. David's, of a college for the education of Welsh youth, particularly with a view to their subsequent ordination; and I notice this point with peculiar pleasure, because it was my lot, when holding the office of Chancellor of the Exchequer, to advise His late Majesty to contribute largely, out of funds at the disposal of the Government, to this interesting object, which I have been most happy to learn has been eminently successful in facilitating the introduction into the Church of well qualified young men, who might otherwise have been unable, out of their own resources, to obtain the advantage of a sufficient education. His useful and good life was prolonged beyond the ordinary period of existence; and, notwithstanding the advance of age with its infirmities, he continued, I understand, till within a few months of its close, to evince his regard for sound learning, and his anxiety for the cultivation of pure theology and for the interest of the Church of England, by publishing a great variety of charges and other tracts, both critical and doctrinal. I therefore hesitate not to condole with the Members of this Society upon the loss which we have sustained, and to express my earnest hope that the sacred profession to which he belonged, may never be wanting in men, equally zealous in the performance of their high duties, equally competent to an adequate discharge of them, and equally prepared to meet their termination.

The next loss to our Society, which we have at this time to lament, is that of the Rev. George Richards, D.D., one of the coadjutors of Bishop Burgess in the formation and advancement of the Royal Society of Literature, of which he had been many years a Vice-President.

As no Member of the Society was better known among us than this gentleman, so, I am sure, I only express the sentiment of all here, when I say, that none could be more generally regarded with the esteem and affection, which his attainments, his virtues, and the peculiar amenity of his manners deserved. Respecting those abilities, on which Dr. Richards's reputation as a scholar and a man of letters was founded, he has left behind him no evidence for those who were not among his personal acquaintance to decide, except his excellent Oxford

Prize Poem, the "Aboriginal Britons," and his "Sermons on Prophecy, at the Bampton Lecture;" but the place where we are now assembled is replete with memorials of his exemplary conduct as a clergyman, and his liberality to the parishes of which he was successively the incumbent. The benefits of his attention and his benevolence were not, however, confined to his own immediate district, he was a munificent supporter of many of the literary and charitable institutions of the Metropolis. It is known to most of those who hear me, that he contributed largely towards the fund for the erection of the building in which we are now met; and, for the information of those who may be yet unacquainted with the fact, I believe I am at liberty to intimate, that he has by his will left to this Society still more substantial proofs of his anxiety for its welfare.

The last Member, whose decease, since the anniversary of 1836, I am called on to notice, is the late Sir Francis Freeling, a gentleman whose name is familiar to every one, in the character of a valuable public servant, but who was no less known to many as a sincere lover and liberal patron of Literature.

In 1836 the second volume of Transactions was completed.

In 1837 the Society lost its second Royal Patron, King William IV., and on Queen Victoria's accession to the throne, a loyal address to Her was adopted at a meeting specially called for the purpose. In response, Sir H. Wheatley, Keeper of Her Majesty's Privy Purse, was instructed to inform the Society "that Her Majesty would be graciously pleased to afford the same patronage and support to the Royal Society of Literature, which that valuable institution had enjoyed during His late Majesty's reign." In consequence, the Royal donation of £100 was annually made until the year 1890. The marriage of Her Majesty in 1840 was made the subject of an address of congratulation; and the Society in felicitating Prince Albert on the same occasion, took the opportunity of suggesting that he should become an Honorary Member. His letter of consent contained an assurance of the deep interest he would never cease to take in the arduous and enlightened labours in which the Society was engaged. The Society at the same time greatly strengthened its list of Honorary Members by the addition of the following names :—

Bunsen, Secretary General of the Archæological Institute of Rome;

Rafn, Secretary of the Royal Society of Northern Antiquaries of Copenhagen;

Boeckh, of Berlin;

Guizot;

Thiers;

Gerhard, of Berlin;

Müller, of Göttingen;

Lepsius;

Mr. Isaac Cullimore;

The Rev. R. T. Leider, of Cairo.

In his address of 1838, Lord Ripon communicated to the Society the following proposition made by Mr. Wm. Tooke, a member of the Council :—

Having more than once intimated to the Council a suggestion, to the development of which, however, I feel very unequal, that it would conduce to the efficiency, and at the same time promote the welfare of the Royal Society of Literature, were its Council to undertake or sanction some extended work, calculated to promulgate and perpetuate the deeds and labours of our ancestors, in every department of arts and arms, of science, eloquence, and literature; I am induced to trouble you with the following outline sketch of the nature of the work I would propose for the consideration of the Council. I would, with this view, recommend the publication in parts by, or rather under the superintendence of, the Council of the Royal Society of Literature, of a biographical series, not in the ordinary inartificial and imperfect plan of alphabetical arrangement, but in chronological order, thus obviating the inconvenience of the anachronism which occurs between the early and late volumes of a long set, as is the case in Chalmers's Dictionary, which occupied upwards of five years in publication, in consequence of which notices were given in the latter volumes of persons who had long survived others, of whom no mention whatever is made in the earlier sections of the work, while a still greater anachronism occurs from the juxta-position of men who flourished at the most remote periods from one another, by which means Alfred and Akenside, Wickliff and Wilmot, Chaucer and Chatterton, are jumbled together in very absurd discrepancy. Another defect of biographical dictionaries is the attempt to render them universal, as to all nations, and as to every description of notoriety of character.

I would endeavour to obviate both these sources of imperfection by making the proposed biography purely national, and arranging it chronologically by centuries, on which plan each volume might be considered a separate work. The volumes might even be published simultaneously, or, beginning with recent centuries, work upwards to the source; and, in either case, the work would admit of indefinite continuance with the lapse of time, while the earlier portions would never become obsolete or lose their relative value, as has invariably been the fate of all alphabetical biographies.

The scanty, but still more interesting list of names previous to the invention of printing, would, of course, compress that period into small comparative compass; and thus, while the luminaries of England existing between the seventh and fourteenth centuries, beginning with Bede, Alcuin, and Alfred, and ending with Lydgate, might be comprised in one or two volumes, the materials would soon expand, until the later centuries would each require several volumes to record the histories of their illustrious occupants.

The only attempt on any adequate scale at a national biography was by the publication, between the years 1747 and 1766, of a " Biographia Britannica," of which an enlarged edition was, in 1777, undertaken by Dr. Kippis and others, and slowly continued until the year 1793, when it ceased to appear, having proceeded no further than the letter E. Independent of its vicious alphabetical arrangement, and its bulk and uncertain periods of publication, enough of cause for its non-acceptance by the public, and consequent abrupt termination, would be found in its injudicious plan of giving the entire text of the former edition, and appending an immense quantity of elaborate and controversial notes, after the manner, but destitute of the critical acumen of

Bayle. A "Dictionary of General Biography" was soon afterwards compiled and edited by Drs. Aikin and Enfield, without, however, establishing any claim to distinction in the literary world.

Another mode of improving on the crude and desultory character of all existing large works in general biography, would be by a classification of the lives according to the different branches of literature and science to which they were devoted; but this would be attended with great difficulty, in consequence of the versatile pursuits of many distinguished geniuses, who, like Julius Cæsar, or our own Alfred, have earned laurels in every field of fame.

On the whole, therefore, I would repeat the expression of my predilection in favour of the scheme I have proposed; namely, a purely national biography, deduced chronologically from the first dawnings of British genius, in the seventh century, to the mature, but, I trust, still far from declining splendour of its emanations in the nineteenth.

The most useful form of such a publication would, as it appears to me, be by monthly or quarterly portions, and at the moderate price which I apprehend its popularity, and consequently extensive sale, would justify; and I have no doubt but that some one of our most eminent booksellers would gladly undertake the publication of the work, with the sanction and under the immediate superintendence of the Society, on terms which would not only relieve the Society from all possible hazard but obtain for it considerable pecuniary return, in aid of its liberal efforts to improve the standard and promote the diffusion of sound general literature.

The President expressed his approval of the scheme and a fund was raised for carrying it into effect, the total subscriptions amounting to £580 15s. The first portion of the work—an Essay on the "State of Literature and Learning among the Anglo-Saxons," by Mr. Thomas Wright, was issued in 1839.

In 1838, the third and last volume of the Society's quarto series of Transactions was completed. The principal contents of the three volumes, in addition to the papers already mentioned, are as follows :—

Vol. I. (1829)—
- Part I.—
  On some Egyptian Monuments in the British Museum and other collections. By the Rt. Hon. C. Yorke and W. M. Leake, Esq.
  On Palimpsest Manuscripts. By Archdeacon Nares.
- Part II.—
  On the Coins of Zancle and on the Portland Vase. Both by J. Millingen, Esq.
  On the Demi of Attica. By W. M. Leake, Esq.

Vol. II. (1834)—
- Part I.—
  Inscriptions Grecques et Latines du Colosse de Memnon. Expliquées par M. Letronne.
  Inscriptions from the Wady-el-Muketteb. Copied by the Rev. G. F. Grey.
- Part II.—
  On the Theoretical Music of the Greeks. By Rev. F. Nolan, LL.D.
  De L'Origine des Hindous. Par A. W. de Schlegel.

Vol. III. (1839)—
  On a Roman Villa near Pausilippo. By W. R. Hamilton.
  On certain Alphabets in use among the Jews. By J. Belfour.

On the Battle of Marathon. By G. Finlay.
On the Astronomical Ceiling of the Memnonium at Thebes. By Rev. G. Tomlinson.

The second period of eight years, which may be marked by the close of the Society's quarto series of Transactions, showed a considerable falling off in the number of Ordinary Members, from 244 to 164.

The deaths, in 1841, included Dr. Alexander Crombie, the author of the "Gymnasium," and Carl Gottfried Müller, of Göttingen, Honorary Member. In that year the first volume of the octavo series of Transactions was completed. It contains 31 papers, largely concerned with Egyptian and Greek inscriptions, with monuments, obelisks, and objects of antiquity; with the identification of ancient sites, and with mediæval and ancient history. In pure literature, Mr. Granville Penn's critical observations on the Epistle of Horace to Torquatus is the principal contribution.

The deaths announced at the Anniversary

of 1842 included Sir Francis Chantrey, the sculptor; and Dr. G. F. Nott, author of "Lives of Surrey and Wyatt." Among those of 1843 were the Duke of Sussex; Southey, one of the Society's Medallists; Sir Wm. Ouseley, a Royal Associate; and Bröndsted, of Copenhagen, an Honorary Member. John Hogg was admitted a Member and afterwards became a valued contributor to the Transactions. An excellent address was delivered by Mr. W. R. Hamilton, Foreign Secretary, in the absence of the President.

In 1844, in like manner, the President was absent, and Henry Hallam delivered a Presidential address in his place. The deaths of this year included Sir Henry Halford and John Murray. J. O. Halliwell and Thomas Wright were elected Honorary Members. In 1845, Lord Ripon resigned the Presidency and Henry Hallam was elected in his place. The deaths of this year were Lord Montmorres (author, as Viscount Valentia, of "Travels in the East");

Sir Gore Ouseley, Ambassador to Persia; Granville Penn and Dr. Henry Card, both literary men of eminence. The deaths of 1846 included two Royal Associates, Millingen and Todd; and three original Members—Law, Bishop of Bath and Wells, the Right Hon. J. Hookham Frere, and Sir Matthew Tierney, Bart. One of the elections of new Members, however, was destined to compensate for many losses. It was that of Patrick Colquhoun, M.A. of Cambridge, and D.C.L. of Heidelberg.

On the 29th January, 1846, the entrance fee was reduced from five guineas to three guineas. A second volume of the "Biographia Britannica Literaria," relating to the Anglo-Norman period, was published. On 27th November and 11th December, 1845, and 22nd January and 12th February, 1846, Dr. Patrick Colquhoun communicated an excursus on the topography of the Homeric Ilium, which he had translated from the original of Prof. H. N.

Ulrichs of Athens, and illustrated with notes. At the Anniversary in 1846 he was elected a member of the Council.

Among the new elections of 1847 was another future President, Connop Thirlwall, Bishop of St. David's. The losses by death included Sharon Turner, Royal Associate, and James Parsons, Honorary Associate. Admiral Beaufort, Dr. Mordtmann, Dr. J. G. de Cramer, and W. H. Prescott, author of the "History of the Reign of Ferdinand and Isabella," were added to the list of Honorary Members.

The losses of 1848 were the two Archbishops, Howley of Canterbury, and Vernon Harcourt of York, and Sir David Pollock, Chief Justice of Bombay. In this year the Rev. Dr. John Jamieson, the last of the Royal Associates, also disappears from the list. The second volume of the second series of the Transactions was published. Dr. Colquhoun's paper occupies 76 pages, and is illustrated by a map of the plain of Troy and adjacent country, founded on the

Admiralty surveys—an exploration since followed with so much success by our illustrious Honorary Fellow, Dr. Schliemann. The first of a long series of valuable communications by John Hogg, afterwards a Vice-President, also appears here, "On the origin of the floral ornaments, the Ionic volute, and the wave-line of the ancient Greeks." Birch, Bonomi, and Osburn write on Egyptian inscriptions; Leake on Greek inscriptions; the President, Henry Hallam, Henry Holland, Thomas Wright, and George Burges on various subjects, bearing upon classical and mediæval literature.

In 1849 Henry Hallam retired from the Presidency, and was succeeded by Spencer Joshua, Marquis of Northampton, President of the Royal Society. Austen Henry Layard was most worthily elected an Honorary Member. The losses by death of the year were the Earl of Carlisle and Professor Wm. Tennant, of St. Andrews.

In the following year a large accession of

Members—25 in all—was obtained, and the list of Honorary Members was enlarged by the names of John Landseer, the Rev. Dr. Hincks, Professor Karl Ritter of Berlin, the Duc de Luynes, George Finlay, Theodore Panofka of Berlin, and Quaranta of Naples. Among the deaths of the year was that of Louis Hayes Petit, one of the Vice-Presidents. The third volume of the Transactions was completed. It contains a memoir, 127 pages in length, by Mr. J. L. Stoddart, on the inscribed pottery of Rhodes, Cnidus, and other Greek cities; two remarkable specimens of ingenious restoration of ancient manuscripts in the paper by Dr. E. Hincks on the Turin book of Kings, and by Churchill Babington on a Greek papyrus belonging to Mr. A. C. Harris, and containing fragments of the oration of Hyperides against Demosthenes respecting the money of Harpalus; a memoir, 140 pages in length, by Mr. W. Martin Leake, Vice-President, on Syracuse; two articles on Egyptian hieroglyphics, by

Samuel Birch; and a paper by Mr. Hogg in support of the theory of Lepsius that Mount Serbal was the true Mount Sinai. The volume, indeed, is an excellent one, containing nothing unworthy of the reputation of the Society, and much that was calculated to confirm and enhance it.

The Anniversary of 1851 was marked by a very heavy record of mortality. The Duke of Cambridge, one of the Royal Fellows; the Marquis of Northampton, President; the Duke of Newcastle and Lord Bexley, Vice-Presidents; P. F. Tytler, Honorary Associate; Counseller Macedo and Baron de Reiffenburg, Honorary Members; and Henry Fitzmaurice Hallam, son of a former President, with others, were included in it.

On the other hand, the list of new Members elected contained some noticeable names, including three men destined to be Lord Chancellors—Sir Wm. Page Wood, the Solicitor-General, afterwards Lord Hatherley; Richard

Bethell, afterwards Lord Westbury; and Hugh MacCalmont, afterwards Earl, Cairns; three men of high constructive skill—Robert Stephenson, Thomas Grissell, and William Cubitt; two men who have since earned high reputation in the Society's own special province—Sir Henry Rawlinson and Sir Charles T. Newton; and one man who was himself to be for many years the real guiding spirit of the Society—William Sandys Wright Vaux. The new President, elected in succession to Lord Northampton, was George William Frederick, Earl of Carlisle. At this meeting it was announced that Dr. Richards' munificently meant bequest of £5,000 had at last produced £1,692 only, which had been duly invested. Among the presents to the library had been a copy of his "Summary of the Roman Civil Law," from Dr. P. Colquhoun. The Society, with a speedy recognition of talent and the prospect of future usefulness, which has in a singular manner marked its proceedings, elected W. S. W. Vaux a member of its Council.

The obituary of 1852 included the Earl of Clare; Dr. John Lingard, Honorary Associate; and Isaac Cullimore and John Landseer, Honorary Members. The new elections included a name which remains with us in an honoured place among our Vice-Presidents—Major (now General Sir Collingwood) Dickson, who adds to his many claims to respect the rare distinction of the Victoria Cross for valour gained, as the official record puts it, by his coolness and contempt of danger while under the enemy's fire at Sebastopol. Lopez de Cordoba, Thiersch, and Lenormant were elected Honorary Members. On the 17th December, 1851, Dr. Colquhoun read a paper on the topography of ancient Cyzicus, and on 18th February, 1852, on Dr. Mordtmann's discoveries of the sites of ancient cities in Asia Minor. On April 14th, Vaux read his first paper, which was on Col. Rawlinson's last discoveries in the interpretation of the Assyrian inscriptions. In this year the Rev. R. Cattermole retired from the office of Secretary, which he had filled during the whole 29 years of the Society's existence. Mr. Vaux was elected to occupy his place, which he did for a period equally long; Dr. Patrick Colquhoun was elected Librarian, and Mr. John Hogg, Foreign Secretary. The number of Ordinary Members was at this time 173, being a slight recovery from that of 1839, but falling far short of the high-water mark of 1831.

The remarks of the new President, Lord Carlisle, on the Members deceased during the year were eloquent and interesting :—

In the discharge of a duty (he said) which is not devoid of a melancholy gratification, especially when it is, as in this first instance, associated with the recollections and the regrets of private friendship, I have to mention the loss which the Society has sustained by the death of the Earl of Clare. I am not aware that he ever rendered any direct service to literature beyond that of an intelligent sympathy, of which his frequent attendance upon the business of this Institution was one of the indications. He was educated at Harrow, and it at least falls within the range of literary topics to advert to the impression which his character, singularly little liable to change, made, both there and later in life, on his distinguished schoolfellow Lord Byron. I am tempted to refer you to a highly characteristic letter addressed from Lord Clare, while at Harrow, to Lord Byron, remonstrating with him on account of some supposed change of manner. In the course of it he says, "Though you do not let the boys bully me, yet if you treat me unkindly, that is to me a great deal worse."

This was in 1805. In 1821, Lord Byron writes of him:—" Of all I have ever known, he has been the least altered in everything from the excellent qualities and kind affections which attached me to him so strongly at school. I should hardly have thought it possible for society (or the world as it is called) to leave a being with so little of the leaven of the bad passions."

It was truly one of those characters which the

world spoils not. It combined a light-hearted, playful, and most tender nature with a sense of justice, a love of truth, a discrimination between right and wrong, which many a sterner disposition fails to attain. Without any pretension of brilliant talents, he possessed an union of intellectual and moral qualities which made a better substitute for them. He had a sound clear understanding, endowed in a remarkable degree with the faculty of promptly separating the main substance from the mere accessories of a subject; his moral courage was of a high order, because his moral perceptions were acute and sensitive. Peculiarly alive to the attractions of society, to the pleasures of friendship and family affections, and without the habits or temperament which much courted public notice, he yet had opportunities of showing that he did not shrink from the graver duties of existence. When he received, in his mature life, the honourable appointment of Governor of Bombay, he discharged its duties to the unmixed satisfaction both of the Queen's Government and the Directors of the East India Company, by many of whom this feeling was conveyed to him, even long after the termination of his Government, in the most emphatic manner. I should select, however, as the chief and crowning praise of his career, the manner in which he fulfilled and exemplified the duties of a resident Irish landlord: my own past official connection with Ireland, and I am happy on this occasion to be able to appeal to still more recent official experience close at hand (the Earl of Clarendon), gives me the right to speak with something of the authority of a witness on this point: his commodious and well-ordered mansion rose by the banks of the spreading Shannon, but it was to his poorer neighbours that he devoted his judicious, unpretending, unremitting care—he devoted his valued life, since it was to a fever which he caught from his attendance at an Irish workhouse during the unhappy season of famine and pestilence that he owed his premature grave. Neither in life nor in death has his ill-fated country been as well served by some of her more ostentatious patriots.

The Society has lost during the year, Mr. Thomas Hunt, who, educated at Cambridge, and intended for the church, found himself impelled to devote the energies of his whole life, if not to a very aspiring, at least to a most considerate aim of benevolence—the relief of the distress occasioned by stammering. I learn from authority of high professional eminence, as well as from the attachment of his personal friends, that his mode of treatment was attended with the most distinguished success, and that to the poor especially he was signally liberal and kind as an instructor.

Mr. Isaac Cullimore, whose death has also been recorded, was a native of Ireland, and had been from early life much interested in literary pursuits; latterly more especially in the investigation of Egyptian and Assyrian antiquities. He displayed much earnestness in examining astronomical data as the foundation for his chronological conclusions. He published a work called "Oriental Cylinders," chiefly from the collections of the British Museum, the late Duke of Sussex, Dr. Lee, Sir William Ouseley, and Mr. Curzon. One hundred and seventy-four cylinders are engraven in what has been already published, and it was generally supposed that Mr. Cullimore, if he had lived, would have continued the series.

We have further to regret the loss of Mr. John Landseer, who, in addition to his other claims to honourable mention, took several opportunities of evincing his interest in the proceedings of this Institution. I might appeal to the cast of the column from Nineveh, now in our view, which he kindly presented. At two of our meetings he read Papers on a celebrated Babylonian relic, preserved in the Bibliothèque Royale at Paris, called the "Caillou de Michaux." His view was that the representations on the stone and the cuneiform inscriptions had an astrological import, with which Colonel Rawlinson, who was present at the time, was understood to concur. In 1823, Mr. Landseer published a work entitled "Sabæan Researches," in which it was thought that, with a considerable admixture of doubtful matter, several curious views were laid before the public. It is well known that Mr. Landseer was an eminent engraver, and his instructions and taste probably contributed much to the development of that genius in his sons, which the world now acknowledges with such fond admiration.

I must pause a moment longer on the name of the Rev. Dr. Lingard. He died last July at the age of 82. He was born at Winchester and educated at Douay. At the beginning of his literary career he published many controversial works, and an English version of the New Testament. His principal productions were the "Antiquities of the Anglo-Saxon Church," and the "History of England" embracing no inconsiderable span, from the first invasion of the Romans to the year 1688. That Dr. Lingard added the merits of great industry and research to a clear and unpretending style will hardly be disputed, when we find it said of him by Southey, that he was full of erudition; by Hallam, that his acuteness and industry would raise him to a very respectable place among our historians; by Macaulay, that he was a very able and well-informed writer, although they all at the same time feel themselves constrained to qualify their commendation by very directly questioning his title to the praise of impartiality, or freedom from religious and professional bias; the last-named author, Mr. Macaulay, observes of him, that his fundamental rule of judging seems to be, that the popular opinion on an historical question cannot possibly be correct. It certainly might enhance the abstract truth and credit of history, if all who write it could be perfectly free from any prepossessions or preference, religious, political, or national; but as such a result, while writers are human, is not to be expected, and probably not to be desired; it may be well for the ultimate interests of historical truth, that it should be approached from opposite quarters, and viewed under conflicting aspects; that Grote should succeed to Mitford, and that Hume should be followed by Macaulay. It is said that Dr. Lingard had the offer of the Cardinalate from Pope Leo XII., and that he refused this high distinction from a wish not to interrupt his historical labours. He appears at any rate to have pursued his studies in modest but not unsocial retirement, and, however rife the controversial spirit may have been in his writings, it would not seem to have infected his daily life. He is said to have been singularly fond of animals, and the Protestant clergyman of Hornby, in Lancashire, where he spent the last forty years of his quiet and lettered existence, after living with him in the continued interchange of neighbourly offices, when dying, bequeathed his guinea-fowls and domestic pets to Dr. Lingard, "because he knew that he would take care of them." May we not permit ourselves to fancy, without presumption, that such mild spirits, when they meet hereafter, will think with gentle pity of some of the causes of difference and division that have separated them here.

In the year 1851–52 J. G. de Cramer, Honorary Member, died, and his place was supplied by the election of Prince John of Saxony and Charles Roach Smith to the same dignity. In 1853, Carl Seeman, Karl Frederich Elze, and Leopold Ranke were added to the list. Vol. IV. of the second series of Transactions was completed. Notable among the deaths of Ordinary Members during the year were G. S. Faber, Master of Sherburn Hospital, and Bampton Lecturer of 1801, and W. H. Mill, D.D., Regius Professor of Hebrew in the University of Cambridge.

By April, 1855, Lord Carlisle, the President, had become Lord Lieutenant of Ireland, and his place in the chair at the Anniversary meeting was taken by Connop Thirlwall, Bishop of St. David's, as one of the Vice-Presidents. Dr. Hermann of Jena, and Vicomte de Rougé were announced as new Honorary Members.

In this year the Society entered upon a new development of its objects by appointing a Professor of English Archæology and History. The gentleman selected for this duty was the Rev. Henry Christmas, who delivered several courses of lectures. The Society lost James Montgomery from its roll of Honorary Associates, and Cardinal Maï from its list of Medallists and Honorary Members.

In 1856, Count A. T. de Cariel and M. Oppert were elected Honorary Members. Among the Members deceased were the Chevalier de Colquhoun, father of Dr. Patrick Colquhoun. The Bishop of St. David's deservedly succeeded to the presidential chair, vacated by Lord Carlisle, who continued to be Lord Lieutenant of Ireland, and was therefore unable to attend the meetings of the Society.

At the next Anniversary, however, Bishop Thirlwall was himself unable to be present, and

Mr. Benjamin Austen acted on his behalf. The Society recorded the loss of Baron von Hammer Purgstall, Honorary Member.

The new Honorary Members elected in 1857 were the Grand Duke of Oldenburg and Judge Riccio, of Naples. One of the papers read before the Society during the session (28th May, 1856) indicates, on the part of an active-minded Member, an anticipation of the interest which would in after years be so far exerted as to cause the inauguration of a new science, and the establishment of separate organisations for its study. It was by Dr. Patrick Colquhoun, " On the various races inhabiting the surface of the globe, and on the causes to which their differences have been ascribed by men of learning."

An event worthy of record in this year is the appointment of John Ayres to be clerk of the Society, an office which he filled until his death.

The fifth volume of the Transactions now

appeared, and in 1858 the first fruits of the Richards' bequest were made manifest by the publication of the text of the MSS. of the "Orations of Hyperides," which had formed the subject of several learned communications to this Society, and were now edited by the Rev. Churchill Babington. The losses of that year included Admiral Sir Francis Beaufort, a distinguished geographer.

In 1859, the Society lost its Honorary Members—the Rev. R. Cattermole, who had been its first Secretary, and the Earl of Ripon and Henry Hallam, past Presidents. It added several worthy names to its list of Honorary Members — Richard Owen, Horace Hayman Wilson, Edward William Lane, Sylvain van de Weyer, and Max Müller. The last of these names is still enrolled on our list. As the anniversary address was written in the name of the Bishop of St. David's, as President, but he was unable to occupy the chair, it is not a rash conjecture that by this time Mr. Vaux had commenced the practice, which, with a rare modesty and self-restraint, he continued during the whole course of his long term of office as Secretary, of furnishing to the President and reading in his name the complete and instructive obituaries of deceased members, and notices of papers read before the Society, which are a special feature of our Annual Reports.

In 1860, Birch, Conestabile, and Tischendorf were added to the list of Honorary Members, in place of Humboldt, Ritter, Lenormant, and Staunton, deceased. The sixth volume of Transactions was completed. Among its important contents are a paper of 64 pages by W. K. Loftus, on Warkah, its ruins and remains; a notice in the French language by Lenormant on a monument of the Conquest of Ptolemy Euergetes the Second; sketches of Kertch, its larger tumuli and some other remains, by Mr. R. Thompson, described by Mr. John Hogg; a paper by Mr. Edmund Oldfield on the collection of antiquities bequeathed by Sir William Temple to the British Museum; addresses by the President on the alleged connection between the early history of Greece and Assyria, and on some traditions relating to the submersion of ancient cities; a notice by Mr. Hogg of the Annals of Granius Licinianus, as contained in a palimpsest manuscript brought from Egypt; a sketch of the life of Bürgermeister Wullenweber by Dr. Patrick Colquhoun, and other valuable papers.

The deaths of the year included William Martin Leake, one of the Society's founders, and for many years a Vice-President. His biography, written in the name of the President, but as I believe by the hand of Mr. Vaux, may not improperly be inserted here.

He was a Lieutenant-Colonel of the Royal Artillery, descended from an old Essex family, the Martins of Thorpe Hall, near Colchester, who assumed the name of Leake in 1721. He was born in the year 1777, so that at the time of his death he was in his eighty-second year. He was the son of J. Martin Leake, Esq., and of Mary, the daughter of Peter Calvert of Hadham. His grandfather was Stephen Martin Leake, Garter King-at-Arms. He was educated at Woolwich Academy, and obtained his commission in the Royal Artillery in 1794, commencing his active career in the West Indies. He finally quitted the army in 1823, on attaining the rank of Lieutenant-Colonel.

In 1799 Captain Leake was appointed to a mission for the purpose of instructing the Turks in the use and practice of artillery, and proceeded to Constantinople for that purpose.

In 1800 he was sent by the English Ambassador at the Porte (Lord Elgin) to assist the Grand Vizier in the defence of Southern Turkey against the French, and, in company with General Koehler, he proceeded with this object as far as Jaffa. On their way the travellers traversed Asia Minor and visited Cyprus, where they met Sir Sidney Smith, who had just signed a treaty with the French for the evacuation of Egypt. On this they returned to Constantinople. When, however, that treaty was not ratified, Captain Leake again started, joined the Grand

Vizier, and took the opportunity of also visiting and examining a considerable portion of Syria and Palestine.

In 1801 he crossed the Desert and entered Egypt in company with the Turkish army. On the subsequent surrender and capitulation of Alexandria, he was ordered by General Lord Hutchinson, in company with Mr. W. R. Hamilton, at that time Private Secretary to Lord Elgin, to travel through Upper Egypt and to make a general survey of that country. The results of this visit were, a map of Egypt, from the cataracts to the sea, the determination of most of the ancient sites, a description of all the more important monuments which the travellers saw, together with a multitude of other interesting details. An account of this journey was published by Mr. Hamilton in 1809, entitled " Ægyptiaca."

In 1802 Captain Leake again visited Syria and made a survey of it, similar to that he had carried out in Egypt. He then embarked for England, and in the same vessel which Mr. Hamilton had procured for the purpose of transporting to this country the Elgin sculptures. As is well-known, this ship was wrecked off the island of Cerigo, and Captain Leake and his brother traveller, Mr. Hamilton, had a narrow escape for their lives.

In 1804 he was ordered to survey the coasts and the interior of European Turkey, to examine the state of its fortresses, and to point out to the native chieftains the importance of strengthening them; and between this period and the end of 1806, he was occupied almost entirely in making numerous journeys through different parts of Northern Greece. The war, however, between France and England, stopped his travels in 1807, and he was for a while detained as a prisoner of war. Shortly after, however, he escaped on board H.M.S. "Thetis," Captain Sir Arthur Paget, while lying in the harbour of Salonica, and returned to England in 1808 for the benefit of his health. In October of the same year he was again sent by Mr. Secretary Canning to open communication with the East; and especially with the celebrated Ali Pacha of Joannina, and other of the great feudatories of the Porte, with a view of rousing them against the French, on which employment he was engaged till 1810.

In 1814 Lieutenant-Colonel Leake was appointed as the English officer to attend on the army of the

Swiss Confederation, under the command of the Archduke John, and was acting in this capacity at Berne until the close of the war. On this he returned to England, and was not subsequently engaged in any duties of a public nature. From that time onwards almost to the very day of his death, he devoted himself uniformly to what had been the occupation of his earliest youth, the illustration of the history and geography of ancient Greece, bringing to bear on this subject those many and careful surveys he had executed during his residence in that country. Probably no one of the present, or of any previous century, has shown so lively an interest in the prosperity of the Greek population, or has striven more earnestly to make the somewhat careless rulers of European kingdoms sensible of the really great qualities that the modern inhabitants of those once classical lands possess. The untiring friend of Greece in all her phases, the undying enemy of the tyrants who have sapped her strength or rejoiced in her weakness, there was no name in Europe that deserved to be held so highly in honour by the native population of Greece, as did that of the late Colonel Leake; it is, therefore, with much satisfaction I am able to state, that the present Greek Minister at the court of St. James's attended the funeral of Colonel Leake at his own request, to show that, after so many years' absence, his name was still remembered by the people he had so long and steadily endeavoured to benefit. Indeed, all Colonel Leake's writings exhibit the same unwearying affection for the country in which he had spent his earliest, I will not say the happiest years. Our own Society will not readily forget the indignation he expressed so late as November, 1859, in the last paper he communicated to us, at " the German Government, which devoured their borrowed resources, or spent them in objects of no benefit to the nation," and which sent many of these literary adventurers whom the illustrious Bunsen has described as " young men of Germany who make a reputation by doubting whatever has been said before them," and whose object is not so much truth as a Professorship. " One of these," added Colonel Leake, " attained the object of his ambition by attempting to prove that the Theseum of Athens was improperly so called, and was in reality the Temple of Mars. Another removed Port Phalerum to the eastern side of the Phaleric Bay, thus totally changing the position of the Phaleric Long Wall, and the course of all the Walls on the eastern side of Athens."

Colonel Leake married, in 1838, Elizabeth Wray, the daughter of Sir Charles Wilkins and widow of Mr. Marsden. He was member of many literary and scientific societies, and was admitted to the Dilettanti in 1815. He was a Fellow of the Royal Society, Vice-President of this Society, an Honorary Member of the Royal Academy of Sciences at Berlin, and a corresponding Member of the French Institute.

Colonel Leake has published the following works: —1. Researches in Greece, London, 8vo (1814); 2. The Topography of Athens, London, 8vo (1821), with plates in 4to.—2nd edition, 2 vols., London, 8vo (1841); 3. Burckhardt's Travels in Nubia, Syria, &c., 4to (1822); 4. Journal of a Tour in Asia Minor, London, 8vo (1824); 5. Historical Outline of the Greek Revolution, London, 12mo (1826); 6. The Demi of Attica (1829); 7. Travels in the Morea, 3 vols., London, 8vo (1830)—with a Supplement, entitled, Piloponnesiaca, London, 8vo (1846); 8. Travels in Northern Greece, 4 vols., London, 8vo

(1836); 9. Greece at the End of Twenty-three Years' Protection, London, 8vo (1851); 10. Numismata Hellenica, London, 4to (1854)—with a Supplement (1859); 11. On Some Disputed Questions of Ancient Geography, London, 8vo (1857).

In 1860–61 Bunsen and Horace Hayman Wilson, Honorary Members, died. The former was a diplomatist and scholar of eminence, the latter a learned professor of Sanscrit. Count Gargallo Grimaldi and Edwin Norris, Secretary of the Royal Asiatic Society, were elected in their places.

In 1861–62 the losses of Ordinary Members included the Rev. Thomas Hartwell Horne, a man who, by his industry and talents, raised himself from an inferior position in life to one of acknowledged literary eminence and great religious usefulness.

Dr. Reinhold Pauli, M. von Kohne, and Count Serge von Stroganoff were elected Honorary Members this year, and the Pasha of Egypt, M. Charma, and Prince Lucien Bonaparte in the following year.

A curious incident of the year 1863 was the exhibition at the Society's house on two mornings in January of a collection of papyri belonging to Mr. Mayer, of Liverpool, for inspection by the learned. They had been acquired by him from Constantine Simonides, who attended to exhibit them; but the judgment of those who attended—among whom were Madden, Birch, Bonomi, and Cureton—was "decidedly adverse to their genuineness." One papyrus was subjected to minute examination by a competent scholar, Mr. C. W. Goodwin, and declared to be a rank forgery, probably of very recent date.

In 1864 Dean Hook was elected an Honorary Member. In 1865 Rafn died, and the Rev. Dr. H. S. McKee was elected. Professor Tischendorf exhibited at an evening meeting and during two mornings the Codex Frederico-Augustanus and facsimiles of the

Codex Sinaiticus. Several notable losses by death of Ordinary Members occurred this year, viz.:— Cardinal Wiseman, Hudson Gurney, the Earl of Carlisle, the Duke of Northumberland, and Archdeacon Burney. In 1866 the Duke di Castel Brolo was elected an Honorary Member. In 1867 the Rev. Dr. Edward Hincks, Honorary Member, died, and his place was supplied by Sir J. Madden. In 1868 Quaranta, a distinguished Italian archæologist, died, and Tribution and van Bodenstedt were elected. Among the deaths of 1870 were Thomas Watts, Honorary Member; John Hogg, Vice-President; and James Hunt, Foreign Secretary. The latter was son of Thomas Hunt, referred to in a previous obituary, and was the founder of the Anthropological Society of London, and a man of prodigious energy and contagious enthusiasm. He was seized with fatal illness at a meeting of the British Association.

Mr. Hogg had contributed not less than

twenty-seven papers to the Transactions of the Society.

Amongst the losses of 1871 are Edward Foss, Thomas Fuller, Sir Frederick Pollock, and Bolton Corney.

In 1874–75 the Society lost no fewer than six of its Honorary Members, the King of Saxony, Van de Weyer, Guizot, Finlay, Tischendorf, and McKee. The first three were as much distinguished statesmen as literary men.

In 1876, Dr. Connop Thirlwall, the President, who had for a few years retired from the Bishopric of St. David's, died. In consequence the address this year is that of the Council, and not of the President. It was, in fact, as all Presidential addresses had then been for many years, written by Mr. Vaux. It contains the following biography of the Bishop.

Connop Thirlwall, D.D., late Bishop of St. David's, and President of this Society, was born in the Parish of Stepney, London, on February 11, 1797. In very early life he was distinguished for a rapid acquirement of knowledge far beyond that of ordinary schoolboys, and for an accuracy of memory that foreshadowed the deep and varied learning of his later days. A very curious little book is still extant, entitled " Primitiæ, or Essays and Poems on various subjects, by C. T., eleven years of age, with a preface by his father, T. Thirlwall, the Vicar of Bowers Gifford, Co. Essex, London, 1809." This book contains much matter of high promise, and is by no means a compilation merely due to parental love or vanity. It is really one of the very rare illustrations of a precocious child, who grew into the man of strong clear brain and retained his faculties till old age.

Bishop Thirlwall's first public education was at the Charter House; after which he went to Trinity College, Cambridge, and, there, soon showed of what mettle he was made. Thus, in 1815, he won the Craven and Bell Scholarships, and in 1818 was Senior Chancellor's Medallist and 22nd Senior Optime, besides obtaining a Fellowship at Trinity. For the next ten years he remained chiefly at Trinity, as College Tutor, and helping his friends Whewell and

Julius Hare to edit the "Museum Philologicum." In 1825, he was called to the Bar, but did not, we believe, practise, and in 1828, was ordained, and shortly afterwards presented to the Vicarage of Kirby Underdale, Yorkshire, where he resided for the greater part of the period from that date till his consecration as Bishop of St. David's, in 1840. During his quiet residence in this Yorkshire parish, Bishop Thirlwall found ample time for the literary work with which his name is so honourably associated —the "History of Greece," originally published in eight vols. of "Lardner's Encyclopædia," 1835 to 1847; a work which, after thirty-five years of busy research, and, after Mr. Grote and Dr. Curtius have given their lives to the same task, is not, and is not likely to be, superseded or obsolete. A little while before he took orders he translated and published anonymously Schleiermacher's "Life of St. Luke," adding to it a preface which was supposed to represent the translator's own views. That they were much in advance of the then current of opinion, may be readily imagined, and it is also certain that views were therein put forward very little consonant with what was then held to be English orthodoxy. The work, however, caused less sensation at that time than it would have produced now, though to some extent foreshadowing the views of "Ecce Homo," chiefly because, eight or nine and forty years ago, the periodical literature, now so abundant, can scarcely be said to have commenced. It was during the same early period that he and his friend Hare accomplished the great work of the translation of Niebuhr's Roman History; and well it was for the great German that he found men in England competent and willing to undertake a duty so laborious. In the letters of Niebuhr, published by Professor Donaldson in the Journal of Classical Philology, we see what a narrow escape he had of having his history handed over to a common translator, or, as Donaldson calls him, "traducer," or of having it cut down and epitomised to satisfy the wants of a greedy or needy publisher. It is not too much to say that, in these works, Thirlwall and his friends (one only of them is left, Professor Malden) did more than anyone else to break through the narrow scholarship of Porson and Dobree, and to introduce English readers to those great continental scholars, who, before the Peace of 1815, had been scarcely heard of in this country.

On his appointment to the Bishopric of St. David's, Bishop Thirlwall rightly considered, that his first duty was to the clergy and people over whom he had been placed. Hence, we have but few contributions from his pen, except on subjects, like his Triennial Charges, of an ecclesiastical character or for an ecclesiastical purpose. He, however, wrote an inaugural address for the Philosophical Institution of Edinburgh, in 1861, and a paper "On the advantages of Literary and Scientific Institutions for all Classes," in 1851, and contributed two papers printed in the 6th volume of our Transactions:—

1. On the Alleged Connection between the Early History of Greece and Assyria; read 20th May, 1857.

2. On Some Traditions relating to the Submersion of Ancient Cities; read 17th May, 1858.

In the Museum Philologicum, also Vol. i., 1832, are four Papers by him:—1. On the Samian Anicæus; 2. On Kruse's Hellas; 3. On Philip of Theangela; 4. On Xenophon, Niebuhr, and Delbrück.

As a Member of the Episcopal Bench, Bishop Thirlwall did not often take a public part in the proceedings of the House of Lords; but, in 1869, he made a memorable speech in favour of the abolition of the Irish Church, being one of the few Prelates who supported Mr. Gladstone's measure. During the revision of the Bible, Bishop Thirlwall played an active part, and, from his great learning, judicial calmness of mind, and profound knowledge of Hebrew, was, no doubt, one of the most efficient Members of the Committee who have been so long sitting in the Jerusalem Chamber. Since 1870, however, infirmities came upon him so rapidly that, on the passing of the Bishops' Resignation Bill, he felt it his duty, as did also Bishop Sumner, to give up his Bishopric. Since that period he has lived at Bath, where he died, at the age of 78, on 27th July, 1875. He was buried in Westminster Abbey on Tuesday, 3rd August, 1875.

By the will of Mr. Henry Dircks, C.E., Fellow of the Society, a sum of £820 was bequeathed to it. On the other hand, the hopes the Society entertained of being able to build a College in lieu of the House at St. Martin's Place, which it had had to surrender to the Government for the purpose of the enlargement of the National Gallery, were frustrated. The Society having spent all its available capital in acquiring the site, found it had no funds for erecting the building, and accordingly the site itself had to be disposed of at a loss, and the Society has since had to be a lodger instead of a proprietor.

On the 19th July, 1876, H.R.H. The Prince Leopold, K.G., K.T., was first elected an Ordinary Member and then President of the Society. This amiable and accomplished Prince was known to have had an especial love for literature, and it was with great gratification that the Society by electing him President marked its respect for the Royal Family and added one more to the links of close association with the Crown which the Society had enjoyed since its foundation by George IV. The new President took the chair at the Anniversary on 25th April, 1877, and delivered the customary address. He was created Duke of Albany on May 24th,

1881, and died on March 28th, 1884, to the great loss and regret of the Society, as well as of Her Majesty and the country at large.

The office of President then devolved upon Sir Patrick Colquhoun, whose tenure of office terminated by his death on the 18th May, 1891, after an illness of about four days. He had presided at a meeting of the Council the very day before his seizure. The following admirable description of Sir Patrick was contributed by Mr. Ames, now Secretary of the Society, to the " Eagle " (Vol. xvi, No. 95), a review published at St. John's College, Cambridge :—

Sir Patrick was rather below the middle height; his white hair and refined face gave him an interesting and venerable appearance. Physically he was a very strong man, a worthy descendant of a hardy race. His frame, trained in youth in athletic exercises, as many a trophy of his skill and endurance testifies, seemed able to defy all weathers. It was curious to see the London lawyer, living in chambers, exhibiting the hardiness of the old Highlanders. He never wore flannel, nor overcoat, nor gloves, and his umbrella, as he persisted in declaring, had been stolen by a bishop. For some years he had been lame and leaned upon his stick, but this he treated as a subject for jocularity. His humour was abundant and his wit often suggested that of Voltaire. One of the most noteworthy features of Sir Patrick was the perennial freshness of his mind. He retained to the last the faculty, most characteristic of youth, but always adding a grace to old age, of being easily pleased. Cheerfulness and a most winning amiability among his friends, to whom he was heroically faithful, were yet associated with a wonderful power of vigorous declamation and pungent satire towards his opponents. His manner and conversation possessed the charm of simplicity and homely allusion, which immediately placed younger and less accomplished men at their ease with him. If among the vulgar, who take men at their own valuation, this pleasant and easy freedom ever diminished the respect to which his learning, abilities, and position justly entitled him, the fact would not escape his observation, for among his many gifts must be reckoned a keen penetration and power of discriminating character. Although Sir Patrick attached to himself an unusually wide circle of devoted friends, his manner did not encourage any manifestation of affection; but on the occasion, a month before he died, when it was discovered that the report of his death in the papers was not true, he was deeply touched in finding how much he was beloved, and declared that the novel experience of hearing of his own death was worth having, when it served to discover his real friends. But as a rule it was in speaking of him, rather than in his presence, that any demonstrative expressions of the esteem in which he was held would be used. His sarcasm and occasional brusqueness, though he was usually a most courteous gentleman, would not appear inviting to the mere acquaintance, and made some a little afraid of him; but those who enjoyed the privilege of intimacy knew well that underlying this exterior was a warm heart, keenly sensitive to and appreciative of affection, and indeed some of the kindest words and acts that have ever lightened the burden of life will be remembered in connection with Patrick Colquhoun.

But nothing could be farther from the truth than to

represent him as one of those placid amiabilities, whose tranquility nothing can disturb. He threw his whole energies into everything that he did, and was vehement alike in advocating all he cared for and in denouncing all he despised. I am afraid he had a difficulty in forgiving: "Oh! I am a good hater," he said on one occasion when an old friend remonstrated with him on some extravagance of expression. But his faults make a slender list, and arise out of an original and robust character that must be judged by nobler and more generous standards than the cheap moral commonplaces of the "man in the street."

The Right Hon. Lord Halsbury, Lord High Chancellor, was elected President in succession to Sir P. Colquhoun.

In 1886, Mr. Charles Mansfield Ingleby, LL.D., a learned and enthusiastic commentator on Shakespeare and our early dramatists, died. In him the Society lost a Vice-President, who had, from his first connection with it, taken a most zealous and active interest in the promotion of its welfare.

In 1885, Mr. William Sandys Wright Vaux, M.A., F.R.S., the Society's second Secretary, retired from office on account of failing health, and died on June 20th in that year. For the 30 years of his tenure of office, he had been the embodiment and representative of the Society, and was greatly esteemed by all the Members of the Council. He was succeeded by Mr. Edward Gilbert Highton, M.A., who held office till the Anniversary of 1890, when Mr. Edward William Brabrook was elected. He retired after one year's service only, and Mr. Percy Willoughby Ames, the present able and accomplished Secretary of the Society, was appointed in his place. Their colleague, Mr. C. H. E. Carmichael, M.A., during his tenure of office as Foreign Secretary from the year 1883 to his death in 1895, rendered great service to the Society and the cause of literature by acting as delegate for the Society at numerous congresses in various countries, and by his annual reports on the state of foreign literature.

The following publications have been issued by the Society in addition to those already mentioned :—

Fasti Monastici Ævi Saxonici, an Alphabetical List of Heads of Religious Houses in England previous to the Norman Conquest, by Walter de Gray Birch. London, 8vo, Taylor and Co., 1872.

Li Chantari di Lancellotto, a Troubadour's Poem, edited from a manuscript in the possession of the R. S. L. by Walter de Gray Birch. London, 8vo, Murray, 1874.

Inquisitio Comitatûs Cantabrigiensis, by N. E. S. A. Hamilton. London, 4to, Murray, 1876.

Chronicon Adæ de Usk, A.D. 1377-1404. Edited, with translation, by E. Maunde Thompson. London, 8vo, Murray, 1876.

Common Place-book of John Milton, autotyped from original MS. in possession of Sir Fred. U. Graham, Bart., with an Introduction by A. J. Horwood, Barrister-at-Law. London, 4to, 1876.

Discourses of Philoxenus, Bishop of Marbôgh, A.D. 485–519. Edited from Syriac MSS. of the 6th and 7th centuries in the British Museum, with an English translation, by E. A. Wallis Budge, Litt.D. Vol. I, the Syriac text. Vol. II, introduction, translation, &c. London, 8vo, Asher and Co., 1894.

The Mirror of the Sinful Soul, a prose translation from the French of a poem by Queen Margaret of Navarre, made in 1544 by the Princess Elizabeth, reproduced in facsimile, with an introduction and notes by P. W. Ames, F.S.A. London, 8vo, Asher and Co., 1897.

INDEX.

	PAGE
Acland, Sir Thomas	6
Albert, Prince Consort	45
Alison, Rev. Archibald	23
Ames, Percy Willoughby	92, 96, 98
Austen, Benjamin	72
Ayres, John	72
Baber, Rev. Henry Hervey	6, 7
Babington, Rev. Churchill	58, 73
Barrington, Bishop of Durham	7
Barton, Bernard	22
Beaufort, Sir Francis	56, 73
Belfour, J.	52
Belmore, Earl	18
Bexley, Lord	7, 18, 59
Bilderdijk, Mons.	24, 27
Birch, Samuel	57, 59, 74, 83
Birch, Walter de Gray	97
Blomfield, Bishop of London	6
Bloomfield, Sir Benjamin	3
Bodenstedt (Van)	84
Boeckh, Augustus	46
Bonaparte, Prince Lucien	83

	PAGE
Bonomi, Joseph	57, 83
Bowdler, Thomas	11
Brabrook, Edward William	96
Brayley, Edward Wedlake	19
Britton, John	19
Bröndsted, Herr	54
Budge, E. A. Wallis	98
Bunsen, Baron	46, 80, 82
Burges, George	57
Burgess, Bishop of Salisbury	3, 6, 18, 25, 26, 28, 41, 43
Burney, Archdeacon	84
Burton, Decimus	27
Byerley, Sir John	41
Byron, Lord	63
Cairns, Earl	60
Cambridge, Duke of	7, 59
Card, Dr. Henry	55
Cariel, Count A. T. de	71
Carlisle, Sixth Earl of	6, 18, 57
Carlisle, Seventh Earl of	60, 62, 70, 71, 84
Carmichael, C. H. E.	96
Carr, Bishop of Chichester	18
Carrington, Lord	18
Cary, Rev. H.	22
Castel Brolo, Duca di	84
Cattermole, Rev. Richard	6, 62, 73
Champollion, Mons.	24, 27
Chantrey, Sir Francis	6, 54
Charma, Mons.	83
Christmas, Rev. Henry	71

	PAGE
Clare, Earl	18, 61, 62
Clarence, Duke of.	. 7
Clarendon, Earl	. 18, 65
Coleridge, Samuel Taylor	8, 12, 15, 21, 30
Colquhoun, Chevalier de	. . . 71
Colquhoun, Sir Patrick	55, 56, 60, 61, 62, 72, 75, 92
Combe, Taylor	 6
Conestabile, Il Conto G.	. 74
Corney, Bolton	. 85
Coxe, Archdeacon	. 16
Crabbe, George	16, 19, 22, 27
Cramer, Dr. J. G. de	56, 70
Croly, Rev. George	6, 19, 22
Crombie, Dr. Alexander	. 53
Cubitt, William	. 60
Cullimore, Isaac	46, 61, 66
Cumming, James .	. . 6
Cureton, George	83
Davies, Rev. Edward	8, 13, 17
De la Fite, H.	27
Dickson, Sir Collingwood	61
Dircks, Henry	. 90
Dover, Lord	26, 28, 29
Drake, Dr. Nathan	. 23
Duppa, Richard	. 23
Ellis, Hon. G. Agar	6
Elze, Karl Frederick	70
Empson, William	. 6

	PAGE
Faber, G. S.	. 70
Finlay, George	53, 58, 85
Fosbroke, Rev. T. D.	. 23
Foss, Edward	. 85
Freeling, Sir Francis	41, 44
Frere, J. Hookham	55
Fuller, Thomas	85
George IV, King	3, 17, 30
Gerhardt, Dr. E.	. 46
Gleig, Bishop	23
Goderich, Viscount	18
Goodwin, C. W.	. 83
Gray, Bishop of Bristol	7, 18, 40
Grenville, Lord	6, 18, 30
Grey, Rev. G. F.	52
Grimaldi, Count Gargallo	82
Grissell, Thos.	. 60
Guizot, Mons.	46, 85
Gurney, Hudson	84
Halford, Sir Henry	. 54
Hallam, Henry	17, 19, 54, 57, 68, 73
Hallam, Henry Fitzmaurice	. 59
Halliwell, J. O.	54
Halsbury, Lord	95
Hamilton, N. E. S. A.	. 97
Hamilton, W. R.	11, 52, 54, 77, 78
Hammer-Purgstall (von) Baron	24, 72
Hatherley, Lord	. 59
Hermann, Dr.	. 70

	PAGE
Highton, Edward Gilbert	. 96
Hincks, Rev. E. .	58, 84
Hoare, Prince	. . . 7, 40
Hogg, John	. 54, 57, 59, 62, 74, 75, 84
Holland, Henry .	57
Hook, Dean . .	. 83
Horne, Rev. Thos. Hartwell	19, 82
Horwood, A. J. . .	. 97
Howley, Archbishop of Canterbury .	18, 56
Humbert, Rev. J. . .	. 24
Humboldt, Alexander von .	24, 74
Hunt, James	. 84
Hunt, Thomas	65, 84
Impey, Archibald E.	. 6, 27
Ingleby, Chas. Mansfield	95
Irving, Washington	17
Jacob, William .	23
James, G. P. R. .	. 19
Jamieson, Rev. John	8, 13, 15, 56
Jebb, Bishop of Limerick .	18, 30
Jerdan, William .	. 7, 19
Johnstone, Sir Alexander .	6
Kenyon, Lord .	18
Knighton, Sir William	5
Kohne, Baron von	82
Landseer, John .	58, 61, 66
Lane, Edward William	73

	PAGE
Lansdowne, Marquis of	6, 18
Law, Bishop of Bath and Wells	18, 55
Layard, Austen Henry	57
Leake, Col. William Martin	6, 52, 57, 58, 75
Lee, Rev. Samuel	23
Leider, Rev. R. T.	46
Lemon, Robert	40
Lenormant, Mons.	61, 74
Leopold, Prince	91
Lepsius, K. R.	46
Letronne, Mons.	24, 52
Lingard, Dr. John	23, 61, 67
Loftus, W. K.	74
Lopez de Cordoba, Sig.	61
Luynes, Duc de	58
Macaulay, Lord	68
Macedo, Counsellor	59
Mackintosh, Sir James	6, 28
Madden, Sir J.	83, 84
Magee, Archbishop	23, 27
Maï, Angelo	9, 24, 71
Malcolm, Sir John	23, 30
Malthus, Rev. T. R.	8, 12, 13, 15, 20, 36, 39
Manners-Sutton, Archbishop of Canterbury	18, 56
Mathias, T. J.	8, 13, 19, 40
Mayer, Joseph	83
McKee, Rev. H. S.	83, 85
Meyer, Herr	24
Mill, W. H.	70
Miller, George	23

	PAGE
Millingen, James .	8, 13, 15, 52, 55
Mitchell, Thomas .	. 23
Mitford, William .	. 9, 24
Montgomery, James	23, 71
Montmorres, Lord	18, 54
Mordtmann, Dr. .	. 56
Müller, Carl Gottfried	46, 53
Müller, F. Max .	73
Munster, Earl .	18
Murray, John	54
Nares, Archdeacon	6, 11, 19, 52
Newcastle, Duke of	7, 18, 59
Newton, Sir Charles T.	. 60
Nichols, John Bowyer	. 19
Nolan, Rev. F. .	17, 52
Norris, Edwin .	. 82
Northampton, Marquis of .	57, 59
Northumberland, Duke of .	19, 84
Nott, G. F.	54
Oldenburg, Grand Duke of .	72
Oldfield, Edmund .	74
Olénine (d'), Mons.	41
Oppert, Mons.	. 71
Osburn, W. .	. 57
Ouseley, Sir Gore .	. 6, 55
Ouseley, Sir Wm. .	. 8, 11, 15, 20, 28, 54, 66
Owen, Sir Richard	. 73
Panofka, Theodore	. 58
Parsons, Rev. James	23, 56

	PAGE
Pauli, Dr. Reinhold	. 82
Penn, Granville .	8, 53, 55
Percy, Bishop of Carlisle	. 18
Petit, Louis Hayes	28, 58
Pollock, Sir David	. 56
Pollock, Sir Frederick	85
Polwhele, Rev. Richard	23
Pratt, John Tidd .	19
Prescott, W. H. .	56
Prosser, Archdeacon	7
Quaranta, Sen.	58, 84
Rafn, Carl Christian	46, 83
Ranke, Leopold	. 70
Rask, R. K. .	. 24
Rawlinson, Sir Henry	60, 67
Raynouard, F. J. M.	24
Rees, Rev. Abraham	23
Reiffenburg, Baron de	. 59
Rennell, James .	14, 24
Riccio, Judge .	. 72
Richards, Rev. G. .	. 7, 41, 43, 60
Ripon, Earl	28, 29, 30, 41, 46, 51, 54, 73
Ritter, Prof. Karl .	58, 74
Roscoe, William .	9, 13, 16, 20, 27
Rougé, Vicomte de	. 71
Rutland, Duke of .	7, 18, 26
Salt, Henry .	. 24
Saxony, King of .	70, 85
Schlegel, A. W. von	24, 52

	PAGE
Schliemann, Dr.	57
Schweighäuser, John	16
Scott, Sir Walter	16
Seeman, Carl	70
Shrewsbury, Earl	18
Silvestre de Sacy, Baron	16
Simonides, Constantine	83
Smith, Charles Roach	70
Southey, Robert	16, 23, 32, 54, 68
Sparke, Bishop of Ely	18, 40
Staunton, Sir G. T.	24, 74
Stephenson, Robert	60
Stewart, Dugald	16
Stoddart, J. L.	58
Stroganoff, Count Serge von	82
Sumner, Bishop of Winchester	7, 18
Sussex, Duke of	54, 66
Tennant, Prof. William	57
Tenterden, Baron	6, 19, 28
Thiers, A.	46
Thiersch, Mons.	61
Thirlwall, Bishop of St. David's	56, 70, 71, 73, 75, 85
Thompson, E. Maunde	97
Tierney, Sir Matthew	55
Tischendorf, Prof.	74, 83, 85
Todd, Rev. H. J.	9, 12, 15, 55
Tomlinson, Rev. G.	53
Tooke, William	46
Townshend, John	19
Tributien, G. S.	84

	PAGE
Turner, Sharon	9, 10, 15, 56
Tytler, Patrick Fraser	23, 59
Valpy, Dr. Richard	41
Vaux, William Sandys Wright	60, 61, 62, 73, 75, 85, 96
Vernon-Harcourt, Archbishop of York	18, 56
Victoria, Queen	45
Villiers, J. C.	6
Watts, Thomas	84
Way, Rev. Lewis	7
Westbury, Lord	60
Westreenen van Tiellandt (Van)	41
Weyer, Sylvain Van de	73, 85
Wheatley, Sir H.	45
Wilkins, Charles	14, 24
Wilkinson, J. G.	24
William IV, King	45
Wilson, Horace Hayman	73, 82
Wiseman, Cardinal	24, 84
Wordsworth, William	32, 34
Wright, Thomas	51, 54, 57
York, Duke of	7
Yorke, C. P.	30, 52
Young, Dr. Thomas	16, 17, 24

www.ingramcontent.com/pod-product-compliance
Lightning Source LLC
Chambersburg PA
CBHW021946160426
43195CB00011B/1235